Lyrical
Life Science
VOLUME 2
Mammals, Ecology and Biomes
WORKBOOK

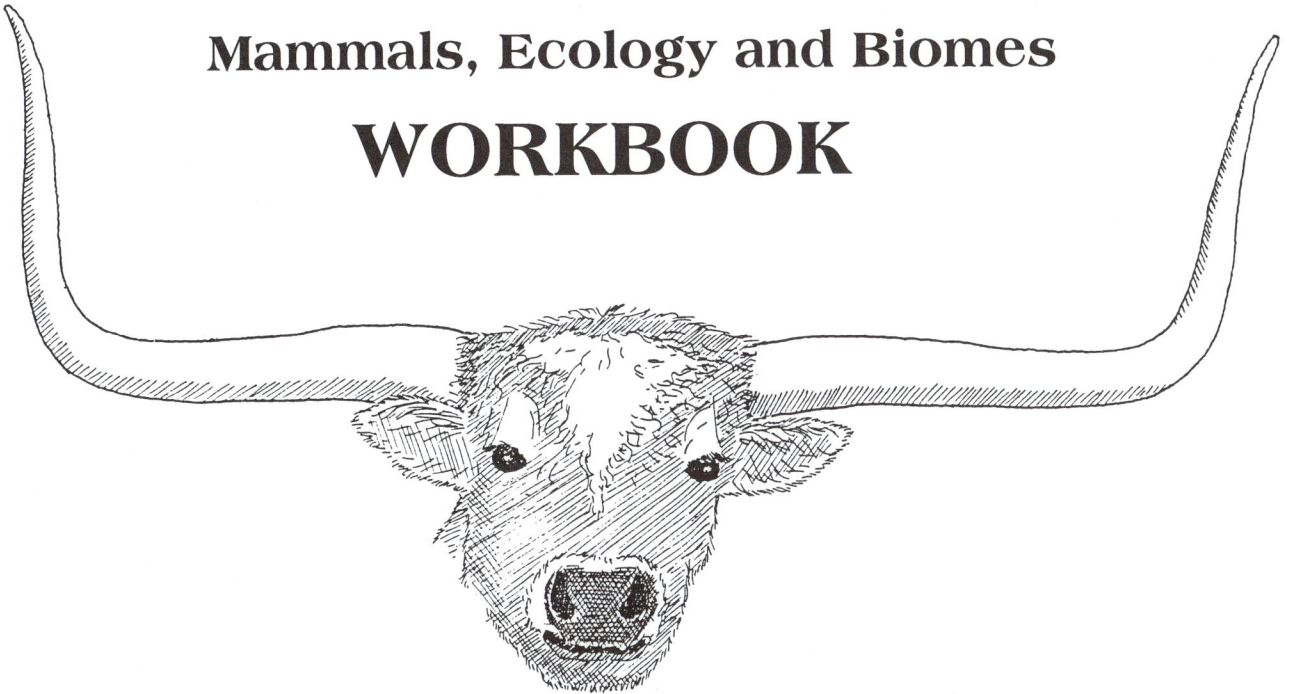

By
Doug and Dorry Eldon

Illustrations
by
Eric Altendorf

Lyrical
Learning

Lyrical Learning
8008 Cardwell Hill
Corvallis, Oregon 97330
541 754-3579

How to use this workbook:

The emphasis of this Lyrical Learning project is to help students of all ages learn the language of life science in an enjoyable way. Because the music and subject matter appeal to a wide age range, please adjust the use of the worksheets to the learning ability and skill of the children using it. (If children are not ready, have them orally tell you the answer, or read answers from the answer key.)

The chapters follow each song on the cassette and are usually accompanied by two worksheets; a third sheet of essay questions is added when necessary. "Digging Deeper" questions involve applying knowledge with deeper levels of understanding and creative thinking. They may also include conjecture in application to relate information to the child's life. Answers provide additional ideas and facts students should not be expected to know.

These worksheets will reinforce information learned from the songs and text. They may be used for review, in which the student refers back to the textbook for the needed information, or they may be used as tests. Above all else, we at Lyrical Learning want the information to retain its fun and light-hearted feel while rigorously teaching scientific vocabulary.

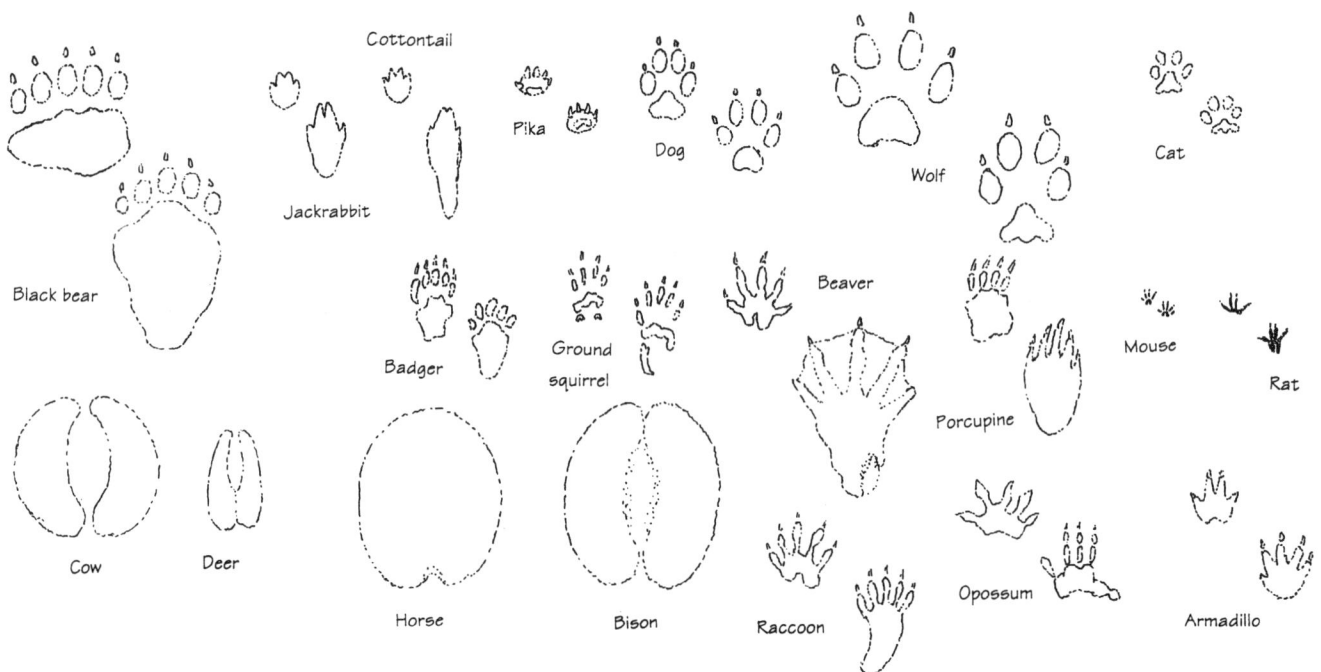

Cottontail · Pika · Dog · Wolf · Cat · Jackrabbit · Black bear · Badger · Ground squirrel · Beaver · Mouse · Rat · Porcupine · Cow · Deer · Horse · Bison · Raccoon · Opossum · Armadillo

Cover design: Susan Moore
Illustrations: Eric Altendorf
Copyright: Lyrical Learning 1996
Reproducible for individual classroom or family use by the purchaser.

TABLE OF CONTENTS

MAMMALS - Lyrics

There are different kinds of _____ but they all have _____ or fir
And the babies all get to drink _____ that they get from their mother
_____ lay eggs instead of giving birth to young alive
And the immature _____ crawl to pouches to survive

There are nineteen _____ of _____ mammals in this class
You can learn of them in other songs but they're listed here real fast
They are grouped by _____ and ____ they eat, how they move or their features
Or where and how they live help to _____ diverse creatures

There are _____ and the rodent-like, insect-eaters and flying bats
_____ and those without real teeth and the trunk-nosed elephants
There are many kinds with _____ and there are water dwellers too
_____ you will remember for the order includes you

Mammals that walk and live on the land are all _____
And the kinds that live up in the trees are all _____
Mammals that live in saltwater seas are what we call _____
There are also those that _____ so high or can glide from tree to tree

Fill in the blanks:

arboreal	how	orders
carnivores	mammals	primates
classify	marine	placental
fly	marsupials	rodents
hair	milk	terrestrial
hoofs	monotremes	what

MAMMALS – Objective

True or false

1- _____ Mammals feed their young with milk produced in the mother's body.
2- _____ Endothermic means warmblooded.
3- _____ A giraffe is an ectothermic animal.
4- _____ All mammals have vertebrae.
5- _____ A producer is a type of mammal that produces wool or fur.

Matching

6 - hair or fur _____   A. place for young to develop inside the mother
7- cheek teeth _____   B. plant-eater
8 - omnivore _____   C. insect-eater
9 - incisors _____   D. pelage
10 - herbivore _____   E. meat-eater
11- carnivore _____   F. front teeth
12- placenta _____   G. premolars and molars
13- insectivore _____   H. anything-eater

List the levels of classification from most general to most specific.

14- _____ Kingdom
15- _____ Family
16- _____ Species
17- _____ Class
18- _____ Order
19- _____ Genus
20- _____ Phylum

Fill in the blank

21. _____ mammals have features that help them move on land.
22. _____ mammals live in trees.
23. Whales, manatees, and seals are all _____ mammals.
24. Carnivores use their _____ teeth to catch and hold their prey.
25. _____ have cheek teeth that grind plant material.

MAMMALS - Essay

1- What major feature do mammals share with birds and fish?

_____

2- What characteristics distinguish mammals from birds and fish?

_____
_____
_____

3- What features are used to classify mammals into different orders?

_____
_____

4- Briefly describe how the reproductive system of placental mammals is different from that of pouched and egg-laying mammals.

_____
_____
_____

5- Describe the role of hair, or pelage.

_____
_____

Digging Deeper
1- Label the jaws shown below as wolf, baleen whale or deer. How is each one especially suited for its diet?

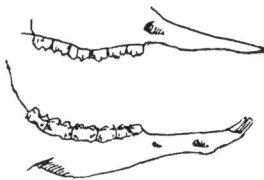

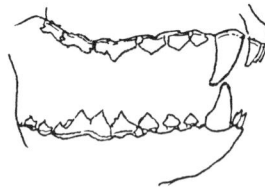

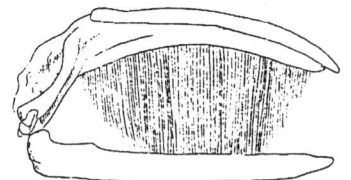

_____
_____
_____
_____

A. _____   B. _____   C. _____

2- Discuss what problems could result if all mammals had the same kind of diet.

_____
_____
_____
_____
_____

MONOTREMES and MARSUPIALS - Lyrics

Koala, _____ , kangaroo and the _____
They are _____ marsupials there's _____ families.

Chorus:
Monotremes, _____ most live in _____
But the _____ have a pouch, and live in _____

The young is born quite _____, it crawls to the _____
It _____ there within, before it comes out
Chorus

Many are _____, others _____
There's also insectivores, oposums are _____
Chorus

The_____ egg-laying _____ live near Australia
There's the duck-billed _____ and the _____
Chorus

Fill in the blanks:

America	immature	pouch
Australia	marsupials	pouched
carnivores	monotremes	sixteen
develops	omnivores	two
echidna	opossums	wallaby
herbivores	platypus	wombat

MONOTREMES and MARSUPIALS - Objective

True or False
1- _____ Marsupials are about the same size as placental mammals when born.
2- _____ Nocturnal means to be active during the day.
3- _____ Most opossums live in Australia.
4- _____ Opossums are the most intelligent marsupial.
5- _____ Monotremes lay chicken-sized eggs.
6- _____ Pouched mammals also have a placenta.
7- _____ The duck-billed platypus is a kind of pouched bird.

Label the following as "A" for marsupial or "B" for monotreme.
8- Echidna _____
9- Koala _____
10- Kangaroo _____
11- Platypus _____
12- Wombat _____
13- Opossum _____

A. marsupial
B. monotreme

Fill in the blank
14- Mammals that eat low-growing plants such as grass are _____.
15- Mammals that eat twigs and leaves of plants that grow tall are _____.
16- A male _____ has poisonous spurs on its ankles.
17- Wombats and koalas have pouches that open towards the mother's _____.
18- Wombats have rodent-like _____ teeth that are ever-growing.
19- _____ have pouches only during the breeding season.
20- The young marsupials are born _____.

Vocabulary matching
21- Non-selective eaters _____
22- Marsupium _____
23- Gestation period _____
24- Prehensile tail _____

A. time in the womb
B. pouch
C. acts as another hand
D. no plant preference in diet

25- Why are opossums such successful mammals?
_____
_____

MONOTREMES and MARSUPIALS - Essay

1- Describe how marsupials are classified. How is this different from placental mammal classification? What do scientists do to help further distinguish the order?

_____
_____
_____
_____

2- Describe the marsupial pouch, its functions and uses. Compare and contrast it with the placenta of placental mammals.

_____
_____
_____

3- In what ways are monotremes like birds and like reptiles?

_____
_____
_____
_____

Digging Deeper
1- With further reading, explain why jumping is a better form of locomotion than walking, or running for the great kangaroos that live in arid (dry) regions.

_____
_____
_____

2- Koalas eat only eucalyptus leaves. How can a diet of only one type of food possibly cause problems for the animal's survival?

_____
_____
_____

CARNIVORES and PINNIPEDS - Lyrics

Oh there are _____ -eating mammals that are known
As the _____ throughout the world they roam
Chasing mammals for their _____
It is what they need to eat
These are mammals that as carnivores are known

They can smell their food with _____ that are long
And their _____ are rather muscular and strong
They have _____ upon their feet
Helps them hold on to their meat
And their lower _____ is hinged to move so free

Oh the carnivores have _____ back teeth
_____ they use for shearing meat
The four _____ teeth are pairing
_____ teeth they use for tearing
Their _____ are for cutting what they eat

In the order there are _____ families
Weasels, mongoose and _____ are three of these
Foxes, wolves, and dogs are _____
All the cats are known as _____
And the others are the bears and the hy—e—nas

_____ are the _____ carnivores
And they live out in the _____ or near shores
Sea lion, walrus and _____
How they like fish for their meal
For they are flesh-eating _____ carnivores

Fill in the blanks
aquatic
canine
canines
carnassials
carnivores
claws
felines
flesh
jaw
legs
meat
noses
ocean
pinnipeds
pointed
premolar
raccoon
seal
seven
specialized
water

CARNIVORES and PINNIPEDS - Objective

True or false
1- _____ Carnivores and pinnipeds both have large canine teeth.
2- _____ Walrus tusks are enlarged cheek teeth.
3- _____ True seals have ear flaps.
4- _____ Carnivores eat only meat.
5- _____ Carnivores are hunters.
6- _____ A sea lion can tuck is hind flippers under its body to help it walk.
7- _____ The elephant seal is the largest pinniped.
8- _____ Canines have canines.

Matching
9- Canine teeth ____   A. cat family
10- Cheek teeth ____   B. dog family
11- Carnassials ____   C. premolars and molars
12- Canid or canine ____   D. shearing teeth
13- Ursid ____   E. dead animals
14- Felid or feline ____   F. bear family
15- Carrion ____   G. hold prey

16- The elephant seal is an example of sexual _____ because the male is so much larger than the female.
17- The _____ eats termites and insect larvae because its jaws are weak.
18- Species in the _____ family, such as the skunk, have scent glands.
19- Carnivores are the only mammals with _____ teeth.
20- Carnivores have four or five _____ on each leg.

List the seven families of carnivores (you may name species).
21- _____   25- _____
22- _____   26- _____
23- _____   27- _____
24- _____

List the three families of pinnipeds.
28- _____
29- _____
30- _____

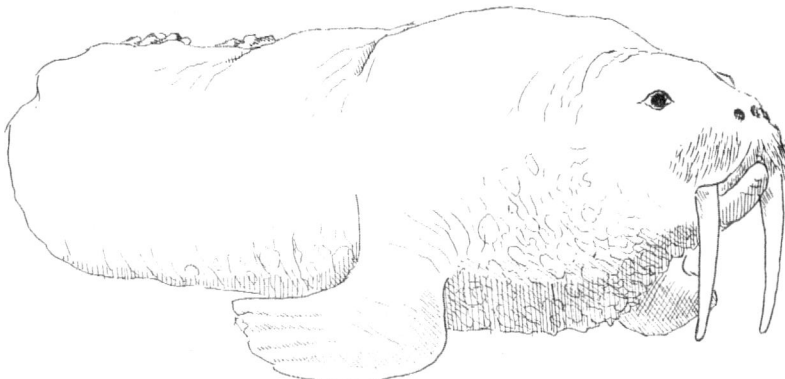

CARNIVORES and PINNIPEDS - Essay

1- List several features of carnivores and describe how these features help them hunt and capture their prey

_____
_____
_____
_____
_____

2- List the four genera of cats and explain how they differ from one another.

_____
_____
_____
_____
_____

3- How and why are bears' teeth different from those of other carnivores'?

_____
_____
_____

4- Describe similarities and differences between the orders of carnivores and pinnipeds.

_____
_____
_____
_____

Digging Deeper
Do carnivores eat each other? Why or why not?

_____
_____
_____

UNGULATES, HOOFED MAMMALS - Lyrics

_____ orders to know
You can tell by their _____
Having _____ which can help them run well
They run on all fours
And they are _____
Known as _____ or hoofed mammals

CHORUS #1
Oh, at home on the range
The _____ where the hoofed mammals graze
When they run in a _____
They are much more secure
From becoming some _____ prey

The _____ can
Be important to man
After years of _____
They help to provide
Clothes from their fur and _____
Meat, milk, and _____

CHORUS #2

Oh, at home on the range
The grasslands where the _____-mammals graze
They're _____
Which means that they run well
To escape being carnivores' _____

The zebra and _____
And the donkey of course
_____-toed animals no one forgets
The kinds with _____ toes
The _____ and rhinos
Are the _____-numbered toed ungulates

CHORUS #1

The order that's left
All have hoofs that are _____
_____ or _____ toes and there's many kinds
Sheep, _____ and goat
Pronghorn, elk, antelope
_____, camel, deer, hippo, and _____

The difference between
_____ and _____ is seen
Every year when the antlers are _____
For _____ do _____ fall
But are part of the skull
And _____ on the animal's head

CHORUS #2

Fill in the blanks,
you may use words
more than once:

antlers
carnivores'
cattle
cleft
cursorial
domestication
four
giraffe
grasslands
herbivores
herd
hide
hoofed
hoofs
horns
horse
not
odd
one
prey
remain
shed
swine
tapirs
three
toe
transportation
two
ungulates

UNGULATES, HOOFED MAMMALS - Objective

True or False
1- _____ Ungulates have an odd or even number of toes on each foot.
2- _____ Ungulates include two orders.
3- _____ The llama is a species of the camel family.
4- _____ Rhinos have one toe on each foot.
5- _____ Zebras have three toes on each foot.

Matching

6- Cursorial _____   A. sheep, a subfamily of bovine
7- Equine _____   B. mammals that chew their cud
8- Ruminants _____   C. goats, a subfamily of bovine
9- Bovine _____   D. a family of true cud chewers
10- Caprine _____   E. the ability to run well
11- Ovine _____   F. the horse, donkey and zebra family

Identify each of the following as "A" for odd-toed, or "B" for even-toed.
12- Bison _____   A. Odd-toed
13- Deer _____   B. Even-toed
14- Hippopotamus _____
15- Rhinoceros _____
16- Donkey or wild ass _____
17- Pig _____
18- Antelope _____

Name the three families of odd-toed ungulates (you may name species).
19- _____
20- _____
21- _____

Name the nine families of even-toed ungulates (you may name species).
22- _____   27- _____
23- _____   28- _____
24- _____   29- _____
25- _____   30- _____
26- _____

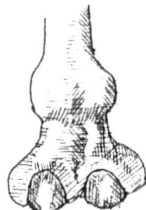

UNGULATES, HOOFED MAMMALS - Essay

1- List some of the ways ungulates have benefited people.
_____
_____

2- Describe the difference between horns and antlers.
_____
_____
_____

3- Describe similarities and differences between sheep and goats.
_____
_____
_____

4- Describe the relationship between ungulates and carnivores.
_____
_____
_____

5- What is the purpose of ruminants' four-part stomachs?
_____
_____
_____

Digging Deeper
Would you benefit by having a four-part stomach? Why or why not?
_____
_____
_____
_____
_____

PRIMATES - Lyrics

Oh, we _____ are the mammals that have five fingers and five toes
_____ thumbs help us to grasp on to the things that we hold

Chorus:
We have large _____, they all face _____ that help us, just for instance
To judge the _____ of things close by and things off in the distance.
To judge the depth of things close by and things off in the distance.

There are _____ families of us in this whole primate _____
_____ and _____ ape, two _____, the loris and the _____
Chorus

Three lemurs and the aye aye and the _____ and _____ World _____
The _____ being but don't forget the so unusual Indris.
Chorus

Human's have large _____ that hold _____ brains we use to our advantage
For problem _____, making tools, the oral and the written _____
Chorus

Fill in the blanks:

big	great	marmosets	order
depth	heads	monkeys	primates
eyes	human	New	solving
fourteen	language	Old	tarsier
front	lesser	opposing	

PRIMATES - Objective and Essay

True or false

1- _____ Some primates have prehensile tails.
2- _____ All primates have opposable thumbs.
3- _____ All primates live in trees.
4- _____ Humans have the largest brain for their size of all primates.
5- _____ Some primates eat meat.
6- _____ Primates often have opposable toes.

Matching

7- Gibbons _____
8- Tarsiers _____
9- Lemurs_____
10- Marmosets or
    Tamarins_____
11- Aye ayes _____

A. live in Madagascar and have long snouts.
B. can hear insects under the bark and pick them out with a long middle finger.
C. have hair tufts that decorate their heads though their faces are usually hairless.
D. are named for their long ankle bones.
E. are very acrobatic brachiators.

Fill in the blank

12- Lesser apes are also called _____.
13- A major difference between monkeys and apes is that apes' lack a _____.
14- Primates' forward-facing eyes help them see _____.
15- Some primates have _____ instead of fingernails.
16- The howler monkey is a type of _____ World monkey.

List the three species of great apes.

17- _____
18- _____
19- _____

20- What do the terms "New World" and "Old World" mean? What are the differences between New World and Old World monkeys?

_____
_____
_____

Digging Deeper
Explain how human beings are unique when compared to other primates, and other mammals.

_____
_____
_____
_____
_____

18

RODENTS - Lyrics

Squirrel, rat and _____
_____ are the gnawing kind
There's lots of places where we find
Mammals of the _____ kind
They move their _____ from front to back
As they chew their food attack
_____ teeth that _____ grow
They must gnaw to keep them so low

Chorus:
They are mammals very small
They are the most numerous of all
There's about one thousand six hundred ninety species
_____, _____, and _____-like, are _____ among these

They've got a _____ behind their incisor teeth
Some have _____ in their cheeks
But they grind with their _____ teeth
Beavers they can change a creek
_____ teeth they use to bite
On our crops they are blight
Quickly _____, a fright
_____ some move at night
Chorus

_____-like include nutria
_____ and chinchilla
Rat-like are most rats and _____
Hamsters, lemmings, and the dormice
_____-like are the prairie dog,
chipmunk, beaver and _____
Squirrels of course and _____ too
mice: only pocket and kangaroo
Chorus

Fill in the blanks, you may use words more than once:

always	gophers	multiply	rodents
capybara	groundhog	nocturnal	space
cheek	incisor	porcupine	squirrel
chisel	jaw	pouches	suborders
gnawing	mice	rat	

RODENTS - Objective and Essay

True or false

1- _____ Rodents' front teeth, the incisors, keep on growing.
2- _____ Some rodents may weigh over 100 pounds.
3- _____ Rodents grind with their back teeth.
4- _____ Porcupine quills are hollow and barbed.
5- _____ Incisors become chisel-like.

Matching

6- Diastema _____
7- Cheek pouches_____
8- Diurnal _____
9- Porcupette _____
10- Murids _____
11- Capybara _____

A. help little creatures carry loads
B. largest rodent
C. largest mammal family
D. space behind the incisors
E. active during the day
F. baby porcupine

Identify the following as "A" squirrel-like; "B" rat-like; or "C" porcupine-like.

12- Mice _____
13- Chinchilla _____
14- Groundhog _____
15- Dormice _____
16- Beaver _____
17- Lemmings _____
18- Chipmunks _____
19- Hamsters _____
20- Guinea pig _____

A. Squirrel-like
B. Rat-like
C. Porcupine-like

21- Why are rodents often divided into three suborders?

_____
_____

22- Why are rodents such a successful order?

_____
_____

23- What is the benefit of the diastema?

_____
_____

Label these parts of a rodent jaw

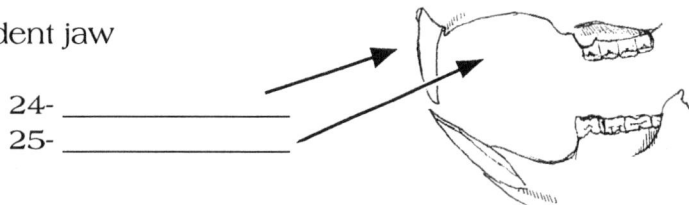

24- _____
25- _____

Digging Deeper

Describe the interactions of rodents and carnivores. Why are the little creatures so important, or are they?

_____
_____
_____

RODENT-LIKE MAMMALS - Lyrics

The rodent-like mammals include these ____ families
Hares with the _____, and _____called conies
These mammals can move their _____ from _____ and side
And on most continents now they abide

Chorus:
The similar genera creates confusion
The _____ are _____-legged and born with eyes _____
And _____ are running, the _____-legged kind
Their babies born furless with eyes that are _____

They've _____ incisor teeth on jaws that are upper
The _____ is the species that is a high jumper
The _____ of pikas are animals small
They have short, _____ ears and no tails at all
Chorus

All _____ eat in _____ habit
The hares have long ears and include the _____
And rabbits include those whose tails are small:
The domestic rabbit and _____ all
Chorus

Fill in the blanks, you may use a word more than once:			
blind	hare	lagomorphs	short
broad	hares	long	side
cottontails	herbivorous	open	two
family	jackrabbit	pikas	
four	jaws	rabbits	

RODENT-LIKE MAMMALS - Objective and Essay

True or false:
1- _____ There are three families in the order of lagomorphs.
2- _____ Sometimes hares are called rabbits, causing us confusion.
3- _____ Rodent-like mammals have four incisor teeth.
4- _____ Rabbits have the longest legs.
5- _____ The North American jackrabbit is really a hare.

List two unique jaw characteristics of all lagomorphs.
6- _____
7- _____

Matching
8- Cottontail _____   A. little hay-makers.
9- Warrens _____   B. rabbit with a distinctive small tail.
10- North American Jackrabbit _____   C. compete with marsupials for habitat.
11- Pikas _____   D. can bound up to 40 miles per hour.
12- European Hares _____   E. structured groups in which rabbits
may live.

Identify the following as "A" rabbit, "B" hare, or "C" pika.
13- Short broad ears _____
14- Longest ears_____   A. rabbit
15- Tailless _____   B. hare
16- Long legs for jumping _____   C. pika
17- Escapes by hiding _____

Fill in the blank
18- Another name for pika is _____.
19- _____ are born with fur.
20- _____ are born without fur.

21- Describe how the rabbits' features influence where they make their homes.
_____
_____

22- How are lagomorphs and rodents alike? _____
_____
_____

23 - How are lagomorphs and rodents different? _____
_____
_____

Digging Deeper
Ever since hares were introduced in Australia they have made life hard for the native species. What is the problem with introducing non-native species any-where?_____
_____
_____
_____

BATS - Lyrics

Bats are the _____ mammals features designed for flight
_____ is the _____ name
Refers to the _____ covered with flight _____
That allow the bats to fly slowly and quickly dart in the sky
To catch flies, eat _____ in the _____ night as they fly

Nearly a thousand _____ and bats can _____ well
Most use a method that's like _____
_____ to know where things are
For they can squeak very high _____ that _____ off the objects nearby
And return to them as an _____ as they fly

Bats _____ seeds of fruit trees, others _____ plants
_____ control to the humans give
Bats return at dawn to the places they live
In the _____ or up in the treetops to hang upside down by their _____
And the bats are really so _____ to man and beast

Fill in the blanks:

bounce	echo	helpful	order's
caves	echolocation	insect	pitches
Chiroptera	feet	insects	pollinate
dark	flying	membranes	radar
disperse	hands	navigate	species

BATS - Objective and Essay

True or false

1- _____ Bats are the only mammals that can fly.
2- _____ Bats can be gentle and affectionate.
3- _____ Bats do not migrate.
4- _____ Bats can reproduce at the same rate of rodents.
5- _____ Bats are harmful to people.
6- _____ One brown bat can eat 600 mosquitoes in one night.

Matching

7- Insect-eater _____   A. vampire bats of Latin America
8- Fruit-eater _____   B. most bats are this kind
9- Nectar- pollen- or flower-eater _____ C. may eat fish, mice or frogs
10- Meat-eater _____   D. can pollinate flowers
11- Blood-eater _____   E. large tropical bats

Fill in the blank

12- The order's name chiroptera means _____ _____.
13- Megachiropterans are large _____-eaters.
14- Most bats are microbats, scientifically called _____.
15- Most bats use _____ to find their way and their food at night.
16- A bat baby is called a _____.
17- Distinctive noses are thought to play a role in _____.

Name three ways in which bats are beneficial.

18- _____
19- _____
20- _____

Digging Deeper

Many people are afraid of bats, thinking they are evil or bad. Why have bats often been misunderstood?

_____
_____
_____
_____
_____

INSECTIVORES - Lyrics

Insectivores are also called the _____-eaters
They include _____ and _____, and solenodon too.
There are _____ families, four hundred six species
With _____ and the golden mole, also the "true" _____

Here's some common traits among these insect-eaters:
Good sense of _____ is what you'll find with species of this kind
Their _____ can be so small, not much use at all
And with their _____ so _____ and thin the ground they burrow in

A hedgehog's not a porcupine but an insect-eater
It is not hard to define, it has _____ spines
Most roll into a ball, if afraid at all
The porcupine so large and fat _____ roll up like that

The _____ mammal that is found is an insect eater
It is called the _____ _____; they can eat meat too
Some can eat their weight in food every day
But _____ shrew and _____ shrew have their own _____ too

Fill in. the blanks, you may use words more than once:

barbless	insect	pygmy	smell
cannot	long	shrew	snouts
elephant	mole	six	tenrec
eyes	orders	smallest	tree
hedgehog			

INSECTIVORES - Objective and Essay

True or false

1- _____ Insectivores eat plants.

2- _____ Hedgehogs and porcupines are both species of insectivores.

3- _____ Some species of insectivores eat their weight in food each day.

4- _____ Moles can sense vibrations in the ground.

5- _____ All mammals that eat insects are in the order of insectivores.

6- _____ Tree shrews belong to the order of insectivores.

Matching

7- Hedgehogs _____

8- Mole _____

9- Golden moles _____

10- Shrews _____

11- Solenodons _____

12- Tenrecs _____

A. look like large shrews

B. Medieval name means "earth thrower"

C. look like long-nosed mice

D. have four instead of five front digging paws

E. may resemble other species such as otters, mice or hedgehogs

F. have barbless spines

List major characteristics most insectivores share.

13- _____

14- _____

15- _____

16- What characteristics of mole fur made it popular in the 1800s?

_____

Which two families include species that can poison their prey?

17- _____

18- _____

Fill in the blank

19- Shrews can locate their food by _____.

20- There are _____ families of insectivores.

Digging Deeper

Shrew babies often travel connected to their siblings and to their mother. Other species travel in pouches or on their mother's back. What is so important about staying close to the mother? How is this comparable to human relationships?

_____

_____

_____

_____

"TOOTHLESS" MAMMALS - Lyrics

_____ live in Texas, south of the border too
Considered _____ mammals, anteater and sloth too
The anteater eats _____ and worms found in the ground
The _____ likes to hang on the trees and view things _____ down

The order's _____, with creatures so diverse
Of course they are all mammals 'cause their babies, mothers nurse
Because the sloth lives in the trees, it is _____
Armadillos 'n anteaters that live on the land are _____

The _____'s mouth is but a small hole of _____size
It's sense of _____ is _____ 'cause it can't rely on its eyes
It finds an ant nest digs a bit and then inserts its snout
It uses its long _____ _____ to pull the insects out

Armadillos can defend themselves by their protective _____
That are skin-covered _____, this is the armadillo's trait
The tree sloth climbs from limb to limb its movement is so _____
But it can hardly _____ at all if on the ground below

Fill in the blanks:		
anteater	keen	sticky
arboreal	pencil	terrestrial
armadillos	plates	tongue
bone	sloth	"toothless"
edentata	slow	upside
insects	smell	walk

"TOOTHLESS" MAMMALS - Objective and Essay

True or false
1- _____ None of the species in this order have teeth.
2- _____ Some species may live in Africa.
3- _____ Mammals in this order look very similar.
4- _____ Armadillos' legs have shields on them.
5- _____ Anteaters are helpless when threatened.
6- _____ Sloths are the slowest-moving mammals in the world.
7- _____ Sloths have nearly been hunted to extinction.

Identify the following as "A" armadillo, "B" anteater, or "C" sloth.
8- has a mouth the size of a pencil hole _____
9- cannot walk on the ground _____
10- can leap straight up into the air _____
11- "little armored one" _____
12- some species can roll into a ball _____
13- can turn their heads in almost any direction _____
14- can eat 30,000 insects in a day _____

A. Armadillo
B. Anteater
C. Sloth

Fill in the blank
15- The Latin and scientific name of the order is _____.
16- Sloths live in trees and so are considered _____ mammals.
17- Armadillos and anteaters live and move on the ground and so are considered _____ mammals.

List several characteristics most of these mammals share.
18- _____
19- _____
20- _____

Digging Deeper
Why are anteaters and armadillos not classified with insectivores?
_____
_____
_____

WHALES, CETACEANS - Lyrics

These _____ mammals live in the ocean with the sharks and fish and rays
The _____ _____ have throat _____ but not the bowhead, or the right, or gray
The _____ are grouped according to their food and _____ they eat
These have _____, they eat the _____ and those with sharp teeth eat _____

Chorus:
_____ all have _____, thou' live out in the sea
These mammals must all rise to the surface for they need the _____ to breathe

The whale has _____ _____ that together make a horizontal _____
It's powerful and it is so muscular it helps _____ the whale
The _____ of all living animals is the enormous _____
And with the _____ it has been _____ until now there's just a few
Chorus

_____ whales include beluga, _____, and the sperm and the porpoise too
The _____ are the killer whales that together hunt the ocean blue
Baleen _____ leap high from the water and they also sing a song
They sing through their _____ to other whales as they all swim along
Chorus

Fill in the blanks:

air	grooves	meat	six
baleen	how	orcas	tail
blowholes	humpbacks	plankton	toothed
blue	hunted	propel	two
cetaceans	largest	right	water
dolphin	lungs	rorquals	whales
flukes			

WHALES, CETACEANS - Objective and essay

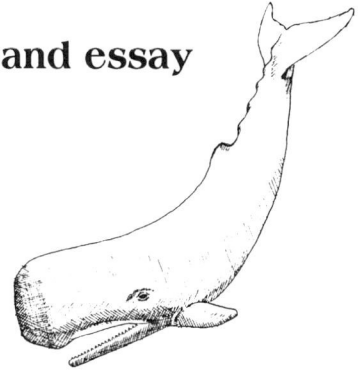

True or false
1- _____ Some whales do not have blowholes.
2- _____ Some whales hunt by echolocation.
3- _____ Orcas are a type of dolphin.
4- _____ Baleen whales eat fish.
5- _____ There are two whale orders.
6- _____ Cetacean is the name of an order

Identify the following as "A" baleen whale or "B" toothed whale.
7- Right _____
8- Dolphin _____
9- Sperm _____
10- Humpback _____
11- Orca _____

A. baleen whale
B. toothed whale

Match the characteristics to the whale species.
12- Blue _____
13- Narwhal_____
14- Sperm _____
15- Gray _____
16- Humpback _____
17- Porpoise _____
18- Orca _____

A. deepest diver and largest toothed whale
B. similar to dolphins but has a blunt nose and no beak
C. also called killer whales
D. males have a single long tusk
E. largest whale, largest mammal
F. has long wing-like flippers
G. has the longest migration of any mammal

Fill in the blank
19- Whales have two _____ that comprise the tail.
20- Whales' _____ insulates them from cold water temperatures.
21- Baleen whales are also called _____ _____ because the baleen filters the water.
22- Baleen is also called _____ and was used in women's corsets long ago.

What are the major characteristics of rorquals?
23- _____
24- _____
25- _____

Digging Deeper
1- What products did whales provide that made them so valuable to hunt? Are these products still important, or are there substitutes for them now?

_____
_____
_____
_____
_____
_____

SIRENIANS - Lyrics

This order has two _____
Sea cow or _____, and _____
They live in rivers, coastal seas
On only _____ plants they feed

Chorus:
Slowly moving _____
_____ bodied mammals
Such unique animals
_____ water mammals

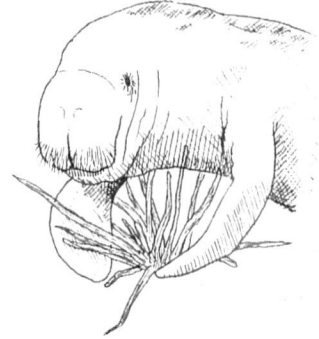

The order is _____
Their bodies, heavy but they swim
With _____ flippers, but they don't have fins
They may _____ the water floor with them
Chorus

_____ thought they looked like _____
So they named them for those _____
Drawing all to shores nearby them
In _____ or _____ water they swim
Chorus

Fill in the blank:		
dugong	mammals	Sirenian
families	manatee	sirens
fresh	mermaids	two
heavy	sailors	walk
herbivorous	salt	water

SIRENIANS–SEA COW, DUGONG AND MANATEE
Objective and Essay

True or false
1- _____ Sea cows were a rich source of blubber.
2- _____ Sirenians eat algae.
3- _____ Christopher Columbus saw mermaids.
4- _____ Manatees may live in small herds.
5- _____ Manatees have been called "big beavers."

Identify the following as characteristics of "A" manatee, "B" dugong, or "C" Steller's Sea Cow.

6- the only cold water sirenian____
7- has a paddle-shaped tail ____
8- has a notched tail ____
9- lives in saltwater ____
10- lives off the coast of Florida ____

A. Manatee
B. Dugong
C. Steller's Sea cow

Fill in the blank
11- Sirenians close their eyes with a ring of _____.
12- Sirenians swim through the water powered by their _____.
13- Sirenians have a _____ -taste sense.
14- Manatees have sensitive _____ that can sense current changes.

15- Discuss why "sirenian" became this order's name. Why is it a fitting name?
_____
_____
_____
_____

Digging Deeper
1- Humans and other mammals have hollow bones, but sirenians have solid, dense bones. Why do sirenians have these kind of bones? What would it be like if you had these kind of bones?
_____
_____
_____
_____

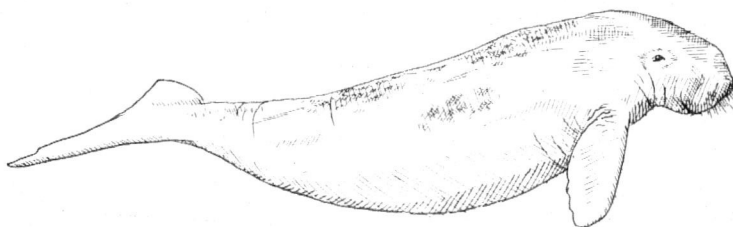

SINGLE-FAMILY ORDERS - Lyrics

These mammals are the orders that have only _____ _____
Combining them all in this song finishes mammal study
These mammals have _____ in common this I must repeat
They're single-family orders that have 4 legs and 4 feet.

The _____ have ivory tusks and massive body size.
The _____ make eating easier because they can reach up high
The _____ is one type of two kinds of the elephant
The _____ has larger _____ shaped like that _____

The _____ is also called the _____ anteater
Protective coated _____ help to defend this strange creature
The _____is a creature rare it has long ears and snout
It puts it into _____ nests and then it pulls them out

The flying _____ looks like a bat but it can't really fly
It leaps from tree to treetop as along the air it _____
The _____ look like rodents except for their front teeth
_____ triangular _____; and they've _____ pads on their feet

Just recently the _____ shrew; also the tree _____
Have been reclassified now each has its _____ order too.
Don't let these mammals be forgot, hold them in your mem'ry
As orders that are special 'cause they have just _____ family

---

Fill in the blank, you may use words more than once:

aardvark	elephants	little	shrew
African	family	one	spaced
Asian	incisors	own	sweat
continent	hyraxes	pangolin	termite
ears	glides	plates	trunks
elephant	lemur	scaly	

SINGLE-FAMILY ORDERS - Objective and Essay

True or false

1- _____ Flying lemurs are a type of primate, a species of true lemur.

2- _____ Hyraxes have triangle-shaped incisors.

3- _____ The elephant is the largest land mammal.

4- _____ An elephant's trunk may weigh as much as 300 pounds.

Matching

5- Elephant _____
6- Pangolin _____
7- Aardvark _____
8- Flying lemur _____
9- Hyrax _____
10- Elephant shrew _____
11- Tree shrew _____

A. also called "little brother of the elephant"
B. scaly anteater
C. whiskerless snout; looks like a squirrel
D. has a flexible snout like the elephant
E. also called "ant bear" and "earth pig"
F. glides by the fold of skin between arms and legs
G. pachyderm

Fill in the blank

12- Hyraxes have a large _____ between their incisors.

13- _____ is another name for the flying lemur.

14- The pangolin's tongue is connected by muscles to the _____.

15- Hyraxes have _____ _____ on their feet.

Digging Deeper

1- If the following species were not classified into separate orders, in what orders would you classify them? Give reasons and support your answer.

Elephants - _____

_____

Pangolins- _____

_____

Hyraxes- _____

_____

Aardvarks- _____

_____

Flying lemurs- _____

_____

2- Elephants have a large impact on their environment. Why are they beneficial even though they trample and eat their way through so much vegetation? What happens when elephants are confined to relatively small areas? What could happen to the plant and animal life if elephants were not around?

_____

_____

_____

_____

_____

_____

_____

ECOLOGY - Lyrics

_____ is scientific study
Of _____ and interactions, you see,
Of _____ things one with another as well
As with their environment, where they all dwell
Singing ecolo-gy colo-gy cology

The _____ and nonliving environment
Are _____ which are all _____
A _____ is all the organisms
That live together in an _____
Singing ecolo-gy colo-gy cology

A group of the _____ kind of living thing
In the same area is the _____
The number that's found of that _____ species
Is known as the population _____
Singing ecolo-gy colo-gy cology

A _____ is a place where it is good
For a _____ thing to find its shelter and food
But the way that it lives and the things that it does
Creates the particular _____ that it has
Singing ecolo-gy cology cology

Relationships include _____
The _____ with _____ in ecosystems
And with the environment to stay alive
Competing for the basic _____ to survive
Singing ecolo-gy colo-gy cology

_____ is predators killing what they
Will then _____ which is known as their prey
This relationship doesn't just benefit one
For predators help control _____
Singing ecolo-gy colo-gy cology

Living together is _____
Where one or more organisms _____
_____ helps one, mutual helps them both
_____ benefit at expense of their hosts
Singing ecolo-gy colo-gy cology

Fill in the blanks, you may use words more than once:

benefit	ecology	needs	predation
commensal	ecosystem	niche	relationships
community	factors	others	same
competition	habitat	parasites	struggle
consume	interdependent	population	symbiosis
density	living	populations	

ECOLOGY - Objective and Essay

True or false
1- _____ "Survival of the fittest" means the most able to compete will survive.
2- _____ To compete means to be the fastest runner in an ecosystem.
3- _____ Predators are important for population control of many species.
4- _____ An ecosystem is comprised of interacting living and nonliving things.
5- _____ Animals prey when they are being chased.

Match
6- Habitat _____   A. the living things in an ecosystem
7- Population _____   B. the part an organism plays in a community
8- Biotic factors _____   C. all of one kind of organism in a given area
9- Community _____   D. all of the living organisms interacting in an
10- Niche _____   ecosystem
                            E. an animal's home

Fill in the blank
11- The word _____ means "together life."
12- The _____ includes all living and nonliving things in a particular area.
13- Environmental factors are the _____ and _____ factors.
14- Factors which depend on one another are said to be _____.
15- The population density is the _____of one species in an area.

More matching
16- commensal _____   A. relationship in which both organisms benefit
17- mutual _____   B. relationship in which one benefits and the other
18- parasitic _____   is harmed
                            C. relationship in which one benefits and the other
                               is neither harmed nor helped

19- Describe how an animal can be an organism and a habitat at the same time.
_____
_____

20- Describe a place that can be a habitat, a community and an ecosystem at the same time.
_____
_____
_____
_____

Digging Deeper
Discuss what kind of symbiotic relationship each of the following is:
1- Head lice on humans _____
2- Lichen _____
3- Humans with egg-laying chickens _____
4- Humans with dairy cattle _____

ECOLOGY PART 2 - Lyrics

_____ make the food and they are _____
Animals that eat them are _____
Eaters of _____ things are _____
Bacteria and fungi are _____

Chorus:
Ecologic'ly the energy flows
Round and again the _____ goes
From the sun to _____
To interdependent _____

The plant-eaters are the _____
The meat-eaters are the _____
If they eat both then they're _____
And that is what you and I are, of course
Chorus

Falling water is _____
Liquid to gas is _____
Which from a plant leaf is _____
And turning back to clouds is _____
Chorus

There's _____ involving _____
Carbon dioxide and _____
Loose in the _____ and then
In soil, plants, animals and back again
Chorus

Fill in the blank, you may use words more than once:

atmosphere	cycle	herbivores	plants
autotrophs	cycles	heterotrophs	precipitation
carnivores	dead	nitrogen	producers
condensation	decomposers	omnivores	scavengers
consumers	evaporation	oxygen	transpiration

ECOLOGY PART 2 - Objective and Essay

True or false
1- _____ Herbivores also eat meat.
2- _____ Consumers and decomposers cannot make their own food.
3- _____ Energy cycles describe the flow of energy among plants and organisms.
4- _____ Molecules made up of carbon, hydrogen and oxygen are carbohydrates.
5- _____ Carbon dioxide is a by-product of respiration.
6- _____ The process of liquid changing to gas is called photosynthesis.

Matching
7- Autotrophs _____
8- Respiration _____
9- Photosynthesis _____
10- Decomposers _____
11- Heterotrophs _____
12- Scavengers _____

A. the process by which plants make food
B. break down dead plants and animals
C. make their own food
D. the process by which plants break down carbohydrates
E. animals that eat dead things
F. cannot make their own food

Fill in the blank
13- _____ are also called "food factories because they make food.
14- Nitrogen is made available to plants naturally by _____-fixing bacteria.
15- Nitrogen is freed into the atmosphere by _____ bacteria.
16- The air temperature at which water vapor condenses is called the _____ point.
17- _____ from carbon dioxide is released into the air as a by-product of photosynthesis.

Matching
18- Transpiration _____
19- Condensation _____
20- Evaporation _____
21- Precipitation _____
22- Water vapor _____
23- Water cycle _____
24- Nitrogen cycle _____
25- Carbon and oxygen cycles _____

A. water turning from liquid to vapor
B. water that is in a gaseous state
C. involves being "fixed" into different compounds
D. water evaporation from tiny holes in leaves
E. water changing from liquid to gas and back to liquid
F. involves photosynthesis and respiration
G. water falling as rain, hail, sleet or snow
H. water turning from vapor to liquid

Digging Deeper
1- Describe a food chain. Describe a food web. How are they different? Give examples of both.

_____
_____
_____
_____
_____

2- Discuss how pesticides (chemicals used to kill insect-pests) can become more concentrated as they move up a food chain.

_____
_____
_____

BIOMES - Lyrics

_____ are dry but the temperature _____
_____ are dry, but all year it may _____
_____ get more rain and may be called _____
_____ are grasslands that also have _____.

Chorus:
Oh the _____ are regions with similar _____
(precipitation and temperatures)
The climate determines soil and _____
Which then _____the kinds of creatures

In _____ forests there are conifer trees
Needleleaf _____ like pine and fir
_____ forests have trees that drop broad leaves
_____ are wet and warm most of the year
Chorus

The _____ biome includes streams and rivers
Lakes, ponds, swamps, marshes, and lands that are wet
The _____ biome, the seas and the oceans
Called the _____ it's too large to forget
Chorus

Fill in the blanks:

biomes	determines	marine	trees
climate	evergreens	prairies	tundras
coniferous	freeze	rainforests	varies
deciduous	freshwater	saltwater	vegetation
deserts	grasslands	savannas	

BIOMES - Objective and essay

True or false
1- _____ "Arid" refers to a dry climate.
2- _____ The diversity of life in a particular area is called biodiversity.
3- _____ The riparian zone is the area around fruit orchards.
4- _____ The soil of a region affects the climate of that region.
5- _____ Grasslands are important to humans because many grasses are food crops

Match the biomes.
6- Tundra _____   A. lakes and all kinds of wetlands
7- Grasslands _____   B. not as dry as a desert, no trees
8- Coniferous forest _____   C. warm and very wet almost all year
9- Freshwater _____   D. less than 10 inches of annual precipitation.
10- Marine _____   E. needleleaf evergreens like pine and fir grow here
11- Tropical Rainforest _____   F. broadleaf trees that drop their leaves grow here
12- Deciduous forest _____   G. cold and dry
13- Desert _____   H. estuaries, tidal zone and open oceans

Fill in the blank
14- _____ is weather over a long period of time.
15- Plants that grow naturally without human involvement are _____ vegetation.
16- Plants that are grown with human help are called _____.
17- Plants that reseed themselves each year are called _____.
18- Plants that resprout from the roots each year are called _____.
19- Grasslands with trees are called _____.
20- Thick woody vines that climb up tree trunks in the rainforest are called _____.
21- Grasslands may be called _____ in the United States and _____ in Asia.

Match the types of plants or vegetation with the biome where they would likely grow.
22- Redwood _____   A. desert
23- Maple _____   B. marine
24- Cacti _____   C. grassland
25- Maize _____   D. coniferous forest
26- Kelp _____   E. deciduous forest
27- Mangrove _____ F. tropical forest
28- Strangler fig _____   G freshwater biome

Name the two different types of rainforests
29- _____
30- _____

Digging Deeper
In what ways are people affected by the biomes in which they live? What control do they have on those effect?

_____
_____
_____
_____

ANSWER KEY

P. 4 MAMMALS - Lyrics

There are different kinds of <u>mammals</u>
    but they all have <u>hair</u> or fir
And the babies all get to drink <u>milk</u>
    that they get from their mother
<u>Monotremes</u> lay eggs instead of
    giving birth to young alive
And the immature <u>marsupials</u>
    crawl to pouches to survive

There are nineteen <u>orders</u> of <u>placental</u>
    mammals in this class
You can learn of them in other songs
    but they're listed here real fast
They are grouped by <u>how</u> and <u>what</u> they eat,
    how they move or their features
Or where and how they live help to
    <u>classify</u> diverse creatures

There are <u>rodents</u> and the rodent-like,
    insect-eaters and flying bats
<u>Carnivores</u> and those without real teeth
    and the trunk-nosed elephants
There are many kinds with <u>hoofs</u>
    and there are water dwellers too
<u>Primates</u> you will remember for
    the order includes you

Mammals that walk and live on the land
    are all <u>terrestrial</u>
And the kinds that live up in the trees
    are all <u>arboreal</u>
Mammals that live in saltwater seas
    are what we call <u>marine</u>
There are also those that <u>fly</u> so high
    or can glide from tree to tree

P. 5	6 - D	14 - 1	21 - Terrestrial
1 - T	7 - G	15 - 5	22 - Arboreal
2 - T	8 - H	16 - 7	23 - marine
3 - F	9 - F	17 - 3	24 - canine
4 - T	10 - B	18 - 4	25 - Herbivores
5 - F	11 - E	19 - 6	
	12 - A	20 - 2	
	13 - C		

P. 6

1 - Birds, fish and mammals all have vertebrae, or backbones.

2 - Mammals are warmblooded and birds are warmblooded but fish are coldblooded. Mammals have hair instead of feathers or scales. Mammal young are born alive after developing in the placenta. They do not hatch from eggs like birds and fish (except monotremes).

3 - Mammals are classified by jaw structure, teeth configuration, type of teeth, diet, means of locomotion and where they live, (such as in water, on land, or in trees).

4 - Placental mammals have developed in the placenta by the time they are born. Pouched mammals are only partially developed after a short gestation period in the placenta. They live in the pouch until more fully developed. Egg-laying mammals are unique in that they do not have a placenta. They lay eggs and may or may not have a pouch for the young.

5 - If mammals get too cold or too hot they will die. Because mammals are warmblooded, they need hair to insulate, or protect them from extreme temperatures. For whales, and several other marine mammals, blubber serves as insulation instead of hair.

DIGGING DEEPER

1- A. Deer
    B. Wolf
    C. Baleen whale
    The deer has grinding cheek teeth to chew tough plant material. The wolf has specialized teeth for eating meat: canines to catch and tear its prey, and carnassials to shear the meat before swallowing it. The baleen whale swallows huge amounts of water and filters it through baleen which traps tiny organisms.

2- The problems would be numerous, but mainly mammals would have a difficult time finding enough food! If everyone had the same kind of diet, they would all be competing for the same thing. Mammals have a hard enough time trying to get what they need! Elephants would be greatly feared, but how could they ever find enough to eat? If all mammals ate meat; how would sloths, ever catch anything?

In the ecology chapter you'll see how plants and animals with various diets fit together in food chains and food webs. They all depend on each other in many ways. The diversity in living things is obviously necessary but also amazing in the balance it produces throughout the world. It's a system that works incredibly well!

P. 7 MONOTREMES and MARSUPIALS - Lyrics

Koala, <u>wombat</u>, kangaroo and the <u>wallaby</u>
They are <u>pouched</u> marsupials there's <u>sixteen</u> families.

Chorus:
Monotremes, <u>marsupials</u> most live in <u>Australia</u>
But the <u>opossums</u> have a pouch, and live in <u>America</u>

The young is born quite <u>immature</u>, it crawls to the <u>pouch</u>
It <u>develops</u> there within, before it comes out
Chorus

Many are <u>herbivores</u>, others <u>carnivores</u>
There's also insectivores, opossums are <u>omnivores</u>
Chorus

The <u>two</u> egg-laying <u>monotremes</u> live near Australia
There's the duck-billed <u>platypus</u> and the <u>echidna</u>
Chorus

P. 8

1 - F	8 - B	14 - grazers	21 - D
2 - F	9 - A	15 - browsers	22 - B
3 - F	10 - A	16 - platypus	23 - A
4 - F	11 - B	17 - tail	24 - C
5 - F	12 - A	18 - incisor, or front	
6 - T	13 - A	19 - Echidnas	
7 - F		20 - immature, or undeveloped	

25 - Opossums have an extremely varied diet and will adapt to the food of neighborhoods, forests, or anywhere they find themselves. They also reproduce quickly and may have up to 20 babies in one year.

P. 9

1 - Marsupials are classified into their order by how they reproduce. If they have a pouch, they are classified as a marsupial. Other mammals are classified by what they eat, their jaw characteristics, means of locomotion and where they live. But in the order of marsupials, carnivores, herbivores and omnivores are all classified together. Scientists further classify them into suborders using the characteristics listed above.

2 - The pouch is a place of safety and nourishment for the young marsupial as it further develops. In this way it is comparable to a placental for an older unborn mammal baby. But of course, a placental mammal carries the young in the womb until it is developed, while marsupials are born immature.

Even when the young marsupial, say a joey, is fully developed, the pouch is still necessary. The joey remains close to its mother to learn all the survival skills its mother will teach it. If it is separated before its "schooling" is finished it will probably die.

3 - Monotremes are like birds in that they lay eggs, and have similar-looking skulls. They are like reptiles because they both lay eggs. Reptiles and monotremes also have similarities in eye structure, and digestive and excretory systems. They also both have unique bones in their skulls.

DIGGING DEEPER

1 - The great kangaroos' means of locomotion, its jumping motion, has been compared to that of a bouncing ball! Once a ball gets bouncing, it doesn't take much energy to keep on bouncing—You don't have to use extra energy to throw it down again. The kangaroo often lives in arid areas with sparse vegetation and little water. In such climates, the less energy it uses, the better its chances of survival. Walking or running takes much more energy than bouncing like a ball!

2 - Koalas are dependent upon one kind of plant. If the plants get destroyed by disease, fire or drought, the koala's only food is gone! Starvation is a real possibility. The koala's dependency on eucalyptus has caused problems. People have stepped in to help these dearly loved creatures.

P. 10 CARNIVORES and PINNIPEDS - Lyrics

Oh there are <u>flesh</u> -eating mammals that are known
As the <u>carnivores</u> throughout the world they roam
Chasing mammals for their <u>meat</u>
It is what they need to eat
These are mammals that as carnivores are known

They can smell their food with <u>noses</u> that are long
And their <u>legs</u> are rather muscular and strong
They have <u>claws</u> upon their feet
Helps them hold on to their meat
And their lower <u>jaw</u> is hinged to move so free

Oh the carnivores have <u>specialized</u> back teeth
<u>Carnassials</u> they use for shearing meat
The four <u>canine</u> teeth are pairing
<u>Pointed</u> teeth they use for tearing
Their <u>premolars</u> are for cutting what they eat

In the order there are <u>seven</u> families
Weasels, mongoose and <u>raccoon</u> are three of these
Foxes, wolves, and dogs are <u>canine</u>
All the cats are known as <u>feline</u>
And the others are the bears and the hy—e—nas

<u>Pinnipeds</u> are the <u>aquatic</u> carnivores
And they live out in the <u>ocean</u> or near shores
Sea lion, walrus and <u>seal</u>
How they like fish for their meal
For they are flesh-eating <u>water</u> carnivores

P. 11

1 - T	9 - G	16 - dimorphism
2 - F	10 - C	17 - aardwolf
3 - F	11 - D	18 - mustelid
4 - F	12 - B	19 - carnassial
5 - T	13 - F	20 - claws
6 - T	14 - A	
7 - T	15 - E	
8 - T		

21 - canines, or dogs, wolves, etc.
22 - ursids, or bears
23 - raccoons
24 - mustelids, weasels, skunks, etc.
25 - mongooses, civets
26 - hyenas, aardwolves
27 - Felines, or cats

28 - walrus
29 - seal, or true seal
30 - sea lion, or eared seal

P. 12

1 - Carnivores have keen senses of smell and eyesight for locating their prey; strong muscular legs for chasing and catching it; and strong muscular bodies for attacking and subduing it. Carnivores have sharp claws to hold their prey and special teeth to eat it. Large canine teeth pierce, hold, and tear; and carnassials cut and shear the meat. They have large, powerful jaws that move freely to open wide when eating.

2 - Small cats are usually small in size and cannot roar. Large cats are big, like the tiger or lion, and can roar.

Cheetahs have small dome-like skulls and unique teeth. They cannot retract their claws. They run after their prey rather than stalk them as do other cats.

Clouded leopards have special "cloud-like" fur markings. Their teeth are unique with canine teeth that are longer than any other cat's.

3 - Bears eat plants in addition to meat. Their back teeth are blunted for grinding tough plant material. They lack the carnassials of other carnivores.

4 - Both orders are meat-eaters. Their jaws are similar with large canine teeth but pinnipeds do not have carnassials. Pinnipeds are the meat-eaters of sea and carnivores are the meat-eaters of land. Each has necessary features for its habitat; flippers for the sea and legs, of course, for land. Carnivores have hair for warmth and pinnipeds have blubber to insulate them from cold ocean waters.

DIGGING DEEPER

1 - Carnivores can and do eat each other. Meat is meat whether it comes from a deer, a rodent or a small cat.

P. 13 UNGULATES - Lyrics

Two orders to know
You can tell by their toe
Having hoofs which can help them run well
They run on all fours
And they are herbivores
Known as ungulates or hoofed mammals

CHORUS #1
Oh, at home on the range
The grasslands where the hoofed mammals graze
When they run in a herd
They are much more secure
From becoming some carnivore's prey

The ungulates can
Be important to man
After years of domestication
They help to provide
Clothes from their fur and hide
Meat, milk, and transportation

CHORUS #2
Oh, at home on the range
The grasslands where the hoofed-mammals graze
They're cursorial
Which means that they run well
To escape being carnivores' prey

The zebra and horse
And the donkey of course
One-toed animals no one forgets
The kinds with three toes
The tapirs and rhinos
Are the odd-numbered toed ungulates
CHORUS #1

The order that's left
All have hoofs that are cleft
Two or four toes and there's many kinds
Sheep, cattle and goat
Pronghorn, elk, antelope
Giraffe, camel, deer, hippo, and swine

The difference between
Horns and antlers is seen
Every year when the antlers are shed
For horns do not fall
But are part of the skull
And remain on the animal's head
CHORUS #2

P. 14	6 - E	12 - B	18 - B
1 - T	7 - F	13 - B	19 - horse
2 - T	8 - B	14 - B	20 - tapir
3 - T	9 - D	15 - A	21 - rhinoceros
4 - F	10 - C	16 - A	
5 - F	11 - A	17 - B	

22 - pronghorn	26 - hippopotamus
23 - deer	27 - camel
24 - mouse deer or chevrotain	28 - giraffe
25 - bovine	29 - pigs
	30 - peccaries

P. 15

1 - Ungulates have provided so much for people including: transportation and burden bearer, meat, wool, fur, leather, and milk. Ungulates such as horses, provide us with pleasurable recreation, while others like zebras, bison, rhinos, and hippos provide us with a sense of awe just by looking at them.

2 - Horns do not come off but antlers do every year. Horns never branch but may twist or spiral; antlers branch and their shape identifies the male adult deer species. Horns are made of keratin but antlers are made of bone.

3 - Goats are lean and usually hairy when compared to fat-bodied, wooly sheep. Goat horns sweep upward and back but sheep horns grow from the side of the forehead outward and may twirl and corkscrew. Female goats usually have horns but female sheep are often hornless.

4 - Stated quite simply,—wild ungulates serve as carnivore food. An ungulate's best defense is to run away. A carnivore's hunger makes it run after the swift-moving ungulates!

5 - Ruminants can eat and run and not get a stomachache. They ingest large amounts of hard-to-digest plant material when they can and chew it more thoroughly later. Their digestive system allows them to eat when they are safe and in more comfortable surroundings.

DIGGING DEEPER

You could benefit by having a four-part stomach because you could survive on only grass! You wouldn't have to make a lunch to take to school. You could just sit around chewin' the cud together with your friends. No more comparing who has the better lunch because by that time, everyone's food would taste the same.

Other benefits: you wouldn't have to wait an hour to swim after you eat; you wouldn't get stomachaches when you exercise too soon after eating and you wouldn't need to buy gum anymore.

Probably the major thing you would have to get used to is the taste. What would your cud taste like? It would be a flavor combination of partially digested food and bacteria (which helps real ruminants digest their food).

P. 16 PRIMATES - Lyrics
Oh, we <u>primates</u> are the mammals that
    have five fingers and five toes
<u>Opposing</u> thumbs help us to grasp on
    to the things that we hold

Chorus:
We have large <u>eyes</u>, they all face <u>front</u>
    that help us, just for instance
To judge the <u>depth</u> of things close by
    and things off in the distance.
To judge the depth of things close by
    and things off in the distance.

There are <u>fourteen</u> families of us in
    this whole primate <u>order</u>
<u>Lesser</u> and <u>great</u> ape, two <u>marmosets</u>,
    the loris and the <u>tarsier</u>
Chorus

Three lemurs and the aye aye
    and the <u>New</u> and <u>Old</u> World <u>monkeys</u>
The <u>human</u> being but don't forget
    the so unusual Indris.
Chorus

Human's have large <u>heads</u> that hold <u>big</u> brains
    we use to our advantage
For problem <u>solving</u>, making tools,
    the oral and the written <u>language</u>

P. 17

1 - T	7 - E	12 - gibbons
2 - F	8 - D	13 - tail
3 - F	9 - A	14 - depth or dimension
4 - T	10 - C	15 - claws
5 - T	11 - B	16 - New
6 - T		

17 - gorilla
18 - chimpanzee
19 - orangutan

20 - New World refers to the Americas— the Western hemisphere, and Old World refers to Africa, Asia and Europe—the Eastern hemisphere. New World monkeys have: 1-nostrils that are far apart and open to the sides; 2-fingernails instead of claws; 3- big toes that are opposable but not all have opposable thumbs. Some have prehensile tails.
Old World monkeys have: 1-nostrils that are close together and open to the front and 2- opposable thumbs. If they have tails, they are not prehensile.

DIGGING DEEPER

We humans have proportionally larger brains than other primates and mammals. With these brains we can create and make choices—these abilities are something no other living thing has to the same degree. Creativity and decision making extends to almost every area of our lives —people have developed languages and arts to communicate and express themselves, used tools to build castles and cathedrals; and created inventions to make their lives more comfortable (and usually more complicated!).

P. 18 RODENTS - Lyrics
Squirrel, rat and <u>porcupine</u>
<u>Rodents</u> are the gnawing kind
There's lots of places where we find
Mammals of the <u>gnawing</u> kind
They move their <u>jaw</u> from front to back
As they chew their food attack
<u>Incisor</u> teeth that <u>always</u> grow
They must gnaw to keep them so low

Chorus:
They are mammals very small
They are the most numerous of all
There's about one thousand six hundred
    ninety species
<u>Porcupine</u>, <u>squirrel</u>, and <u>rat</u>-like, are <u>suborders</u>
    among these

They've got a <u>space</u> behind their incisor teeth
Some have <u>pouches</u> in their cheeks
But they grind with their <u>cheek</u> teeth
Beavers they can change a creek
<u>Chisel</u> teeth they use to bite
On our crops they are blight
Quickly <u>multiply</u>, a fright
<u>Nocturnal</u> some move at night
Chorus

<u>Porcupine</u>-like include nutria
<u>Capybara</u> and chinchilla
Rat-like are most rats and <u>mice</u>
Hamsters, lemmings, and the dormice
<u>Squirrel</u>-like are the prairie dog,
chipmunk, beaver and <u>groundhog</u>
Squirrels of course and <u>gophers</u> too
mice: only pocket and kangaroo
Chorus

P. 19			
	6 - D	12 - B	17 - B
1 - T	7 - A	13 - C	18 - A
2 - T	8 - E	14 - A	19 - B
3 - T	9 - F	15 - B	20 - C
4 - T	10 - C	16 - A	
5 - T	11 - B		

21 - The order is so large it helps to understand and study them by classifying rodents into the three suborders.
22 - Rodents have a high reproductive rate and easily adapt to the environment around them.
23 - The diastema is the space between the incisors and cheek teeth. A rodent tucks its tongue in this space while gnawing. The tongue will not get in the way while the rodent is gnawing.
24 - incisor
25 - diastema

DIGGING DEEPER

Rodents provide a rich source of food for carnivores. Though they are so much smaller than ungulates, it does not take as much energy for carnivores to catch rodents. Rodents multiply so rapidly so food does not become scarce for carnivores.

P. 20 RODENT-LIKE MAMMALS - Lyrics

The rodent-like mammals
    include these two families
Hares with the rabbits, and pikas called conies
These mammals can move their jaws
    from side and side
And on most continents now they abide

Chorus:
The similar genera creates confusion
The hares are long-legged
    and born with eyes open
And rabbits are running, the short-legged kind
Their babies born furless with eyes that are blind

They've four incisor teeth on jaws that are upper
The hare is the species that is a high jumper
The family of pikas are animals small
They have short, broad ears and no tails at all
Chorus

All lagomorphs eat in herbivorous habit
The hares have long ears
    and include the jackrabbit
And rabbits include those whose tails are small:
The domestic rabbit and cottontails all
Chorus

P. 21

1 - F	6 - four incisors
2 - T	7 - grind their food in a
3 - T	side-to-side motion
4 - F	
5 - T	

8 - B	13 - C
9 - E	14 - B
10 - D	15 - C
11 - A	16 - B
12 - C	17 - A or C

18 - coney
19 - Hares
20 - Rabbits

21 - Rabbits have shorter legs than hares and so cannot escape enemies by hopping. Instead they escape by hiding and make their homes in burrows or thickets. (Hares escape by speed rather than by hiding and so make their homes in open fields.)
22 - Lagomorphs and rodents are alike because they are both small animals that can reproduce at alarming rates. They both have ever-growing chisel-like incisors and a space between the incisors and cheek teeth called the diastema.
23 - Lagomorphs have four incisor teeth instead of two and chew their food in a side-to-side motion. Rodents chew their food in a front to back motion. Excluding pikas, lagomorphs have long back legs good for jumping.

DIGGING DEEPER
In the 1800s hares were brought to Australia. Since that time they have competed with the native population of marsupials for shelter and food. Hares are able to reproduce faster so there are more of them, which of course, compounds the problem.

P. 22 BATS - Lyrics

Bats are the flying mammals
    features designed for flight
Chiroptera is the order's name
Refers to the hands covered
    with flight membranes
That allow the bats to fly slowly
    and quickly dart in the sky
To catch flies, eat insects in the dark night
    as they fly

Nearly a thousand species
    and bats can navigate well
Most use a method that's like radar
Echolocation to know
    where things are
For they can squeak very high pitches
    that bounce off the objects nearby
And return to them as an echo
    as they fly

Bats disperse seeds of fruit trees,
    others pollinate plants
Insect control to the humans give
Bats return at dawn
    to the places they live
In the caves or up in the treetops
    to hang upside down by their feet
And the bats are really so helpful
    to man and beast

P. 23	7 - B	12 - hand wing
1 - T	8 - E	13 - fruit
2 - T	9 - D	14 - microchiropterans
3 - F	10 - C	15 - echolocation
4 - F	11 - A	16 - pup
5 - F		17 - echolocation
6 - T		

18 - disperse seeds of fruit trees
19 - pollinate flowers
20 - eat insects

DIGGING DEEPER
Bats fly at night, are difficult to see, and are so different from birds or other mammals. Stories about blood-sucking vampire bats have been greatly exaggerated. Books and movies about human vampires, such as Dracula, have played upon people's fears of the little-understood flying mammals.

P. 24 INSECTIVORES - Lyrics
Insectivores are also called the insect-eaters
They include hedgehog and shrew,
    and solenodon too.
There are six families, four hundred six species
With tenrec and the golden mole,
    also the "true" mole

Here's some common traits
    among these insect-eaters:
Good sense of smell is what you'll find
    with species of this kind
Their eyes can be so small, not much use at all
And with their snouts so long and thin
    the ground they burrow in

A hedgehog's not a porcupine but an insect-eater
It is not hard to define, it has barbless spines
Most roll into a ball, if afraid at all
The porcupine so large and fat
    cannot roll up like that

The smallest mammal that
    is found is an insect eater
It is called the pygmy shrew; they can eat meat too
Some can eat their weight in food every day
But elephant shrew and tree shrew
    have their own orders too

P. 25	7 - F
1 - F	8 - B
2 - F	9 - D
3 - T	10 - C
4 - T	11 - A
5 - F	12 - E
6 - F	

13, 14, 15 - Include three of the following: insect-eaters, long snout, small ears, usually small eyes, keen sense of smell and small in size.

16 - It was very thick and velvety, or soft.
17 - shrew
18 - solenodon
19 - echolocation
20 - six

DIGGING DEEPER
    Babies of all species need to learn about the world around them if they are to survive. With humans, both parents are the natural teachers. As they spend time with their children, (physically close but not, of course, in a pouch!) the children can mirror their behavior and follow their example. In this way as the young grow from infancy to adulthood they learn the skills needed for survival in our complex world.

    In most mammal species the natural teacher is the mother who nurses and constantly watches over her young. A pouch is really a mother's helper, it forces the young to near her. The shrew mother can actually have her children "stay in line" (a phrase human parents use with their own children) when they travel holding onto the tail in front of them. The shrew mother knows exactly where her children are. Opossum and koala mothers (and even human parents) may get sore backs from carrying their babies but it is worth it to protect their young and know exactly where they are.

P. 26 "TOOTHLESS" MAMMALS - Lyrics
Armadillos live in Texas, south of the border too
Considered toothless mammals,
    anteater and sloth too
The anteater eats insects and worms
    found in the ground
The sloth likes to hang on the trees
    and view things upside down
The order's edentata, with creatures so diverse
Of course they are all mammals
    'cause their babies, mothers nurse
Because the sloth lives in the trees, it is arboreal
Armadillos 'n anteaters that live
    on the land are terrestrial

The anteater's mouth is but a small hole
    of pencil size
It's sense of smell is keen
    'cause it can't rely on its eyes
It finds an ant nest digs a bit
    and then inserts its snout
It uses its long sticky tongue to pull the insects out

Armadillos can defend themselves
    by their protective plates
That are skin-covered bone,
    this is the armadillo's trait
The tree sloth climbs from limb to limb
    its movement is so slow
But it can hardly walk at all if on the ground below

P. 27		
1 - F	8 - B
2 - F	9 - C
3 - F	10 - A
4 - T	11 - A
5 - F	12 - A
6 - T	13 - C
7 - F	14 - B

15 - edentata
16 - arboreal
17 - terrestrial
18, 19, 20 - Include three of the following: long skulls, small brains, large and long middle claws on forelimbs, presence of xenarthrales (extra articulation that gives the hips support)

DIGGING DEEPER
    Though armadillos and especially anteaters eat large numbers of insects, their other features do not match those of the small insectivores. Their jaws and skulls are different and their bodies are obviously structured differently also.

46

P. 28 WHALES, CETACEANS - Lyrics
These <u>water</u> mammals live in the ocean
   with the sharks and fish and rays
The <u>six</u> <u>rorquals</u> have throat <u>grooves</u>
   but not the bowhead, or the right, or gray
The <u>whales</u> are grouped according to their food
   and <u>how</u> they eat
These have <u>baleen</u>, they eat the <u>plankton</u>
   and those with sharp teeth eat <u>meat</u>

Chorus:
<u>Cetaceans</u> all have <u>lungs</u>, thou' live out in the sea
These mammals must all rise to the surface
   for they need the <u>air</u> to breathe

The whale has <u>two</u> <u>flukes</u> that together
   make a horizontal <u>tail</u>
It's powerful and it is so muscular
   it helps <u>propel</u> the whale
The <u>largest</u> of all living animals
   is the enormous <u>blue</u>
And with the <u>right</u> it has been <u>hunted</u>
   until now there's just a few
Chorus

<u>Toothed</u> whales include beluga, <u>dolphin</u>,
   and the sperm and the porpoise too
The <u>orcas</u> are the killer whales
   that together hunt the ocean blue
Baleen <u>humpbacks</u> leap high from the water
   and they also sing a song
They sing through their <u>blowholes</u> to other whales
   as they all swim along
Chorus

P. 29	7 - A	12 - E	19 - flukes
1 - F	8 - B	13 - D	20 - blubber
2 - T	9 - B	14 - A	21 - filter-feeders
3 - T	10 - A	15 - G	22 - whalebone
4 - F	11 - B	16 - F	
5 - T		17 - B	
6 - F		18 - C	

23, 24, 25 - Include three of the following:
throat grooves, dorsal fin, slender bodies, fast swimmers.

DIGGING DEEPER
   Whale oil was of major importance as a relatively clean-burning source of oil for lamps and for cooking). Electricity replaced oil lamps and both electricity and natural gas replaced whale oil as a cooking fuel. Other whale products such as baleen is not longer necessary for women to stay fashionable. They do not wear corsets which used the baleen as a stiffener. In women's tight fitting garments, plastic is used instead.

P. 30 SIRENIANS - Lyrics
This order has two <u>families</u>
Sea cow or <u>dugong</u>, and <u>manatee</u>
They live in rivers, coastal seas
On only <u>water</u> plants they feed

Chorus:
Slowly moving <u>mammals</u>
<u>Heavy</u> bodied mammals
Such unique animals
<u>Herbivorous</u> water mammals

The order is <u>sirenian</u>
Their bodies, heavy but they swim
With <u>two</u> flippers, but they don't have fins
They may <u>walk</u> the water floor with them
Chorus

<u>Sailors</u> thought they looked like <u>mermaids</u>
So they named them for those <u>sirens</u>
Drawing all to shores nearby them
In <u>salt</u> or <u>fresh</u> water they swim
Chorus

P. 31		
1 - T	6 - C	11 - muscle
2 - F	7 - A	12 - tails
3 - F	8 - B	13 - smell-
4 - T	9 - B	14 - hairs
5 - T	10 - A	

15 - The sirens of Greek mythology lived on a rocky coastal island. They sang to Ulysses and other sailors to lure them to crash on the rocks. (Not too nice!) The species in the order of sirenians often live near coastal shores, especially the manatee that Columbus and his men saw during the voyage to America. Their presence let the sailors know that land was nearby.
   "Siren" also refers to mermaids. The order was named after them because sailors of long ago thought they were mermaids.

DIGGING DEEPER
   The heavy, dense bones of sirenians help their large bodies sink. These kind of bones work in the same way that a diver's weighted belt helps lower him well below the water surface.
   How could it be helpful to have solid, instead of hollow bones? Well, for one thing you obviously would not need a weight belt if you wanted to go diving. Also, with all the added weight, no one could blame you anymore for moving slowly and not getting things done quickly.
   It would be hard though, to move quickly when you wanted to. Distance runners are quick and light, so it is very doubtful that you could break a world's record or even win a race with heavy sirenian-like bones.

P. 32 SINGLE-FAMILY ORDERS - Lyrics
These mammals are the orders that
   have only <u>one</u> <u>family</u>
Combining them all in this song
   finishes mammal study
These mammals have <u>little</u> in common
   this I must repeat
They're single-family orders that
   have 4 legs and 4 feet.

The <u>elephants</u> have ivory tusks
   and massive body size.
The <u>trunks</u> make eating easier because
   they can reach up high

The <u>Asian</u> is one type of two kinds of the elephant
The <u>African</u> has larger <u>ears</u> shaped like that <u>continent</u>

The <u>pangolin</u> is also called the <u>scaly</u> anteater
Protective coated <u>plates</u> help to
    defend this strange creature
The <u>aardvark</u> is a creature rare
    it has long ears and snout
It puts it into <u>termite</u> nests and then it pulls them out

The flying <u>lemur</u> looks like a bat but it can't really fly
It leaps from tree to treetop as along the air it <u>glides</u>
The <u>hyraxes</u> look like rodents
    except for their front teeth
<u>Spaced</u> triangular <u>incisors</u>;
    and they've <u>sweat</u> pads on their feet

Just recently the <u>elephant</u> shrew; also the tree <u>shrew</u>
Have been reclassified
    now each has its <u>own</u> order too.
Don't let these mammals be forgot,
    hold them in your mem'ry
As orders that are special
    'cause they have just <u>one</u> family

P. 33

1 - F	6 - B	12 - space
2 - T	7 - E	13 - Colugos
3 - T	8 - F	14 - hips
4 - T	9 - A	15 - sweat pads
5 - G	10 - D	
	11 - C	

DIGGING DEEPER

1 - Elephants could be classified as even- or odd-toed ungulates because they eat grass and live in similar habitats.

Pangolins or scaly anteaters could be classified as "toothless" mammals. They have diets, tongues and claws similar to anteaters.

Hyraxes could be classified, though not very well, with rodents or rodent-like mammals, because they are small. They could also be classified with elephants because they have similar foot structures.

Aardvarks could be classified with "toothless" mammals because they have long claws and eat insects.

Flying lemurs could be classified with lemurs in the primate order because they are similar in appearance. They could also perhaps, be classified with flying squirrels with the rodents.

2 - Surprising as it may seem, plants and animals benefit from elephants' hearty appetites. Elephants keep several species of plant growth in check. Without them, the smaller vegetation could not compete, and would soon die off. Without these other types of vegetation, particular species of animals could not survive.

When elephants are confined to reserves that are too small for their numbers, there is not enough food and subsequently, the area is "overgrazed."

Comparable situations resulted from the loss of 50 million buffalo from America's prairies during the 1800s. The habitat was "undergrazed" when these grazers disappeared. Today grazing cattle have taken the place of the buffalo in some areas. The diversity of plant and animal life is greater when the area is grazed, keeping the vegetation in balance.

The struggle facing ranchers, and game wardens of endangered elephants can be similar. Both animals need to have enough area to feed without damaging the habitat. The environment is healthiest when it is neither over grazed nor undergrazed.

P. 34 ECOLOGY - Lyrics

<u>Ecology</u> is scientific study
Of <u>relationships</u> and interactions, you see,
Of <u>living</u> things one with another as well
As with their environment, where they all dwell
Singing ecolo-gy colo-gy cology

The <u>living</u> and nonliving environment
Are <u>factors</u> which are all <u>interdependent</u>
A <u>community</u> is all the organisms
That live together in an <u>ecosystem</u>
Singing ecolo-gy colo-gy cology

A group of the <u>same</u> kind of living thing
In the same area is the <u>population</u>
The number that's found of that <u>single</u> species
Is known as the population <u>density</u>
Singing ecolo-gy colo-gy cology

A <u>habitat</u> is a place where it is good
For a <u>living</u> thing to find its shelter and food
But the way that it lives and the things that it does
Creates the particular <u>niche</u> that it has
Singing ecolo-gy cology cology

Relationships include <u>competition</u>
The <u>struggle</u> with <u>others</u> in ecosystems
And with the environment to stay alive
Competing for the basic <u>needs</u> to survive
Singing ecolo-gy colo-gy cology

<u>Predation</u> is predators killing what they
Will then <u>consume</u> which is known as their prey
This relationship doesn't just benefit one
For predators help control <u>populations</u>
Singing ecolo-gy colo-gy cology

Living together is <u>symbiosis</u>
Where one or more organisms <u>benefit</u>
<u>Commensal</u> helps one, mutual helps them both
<u>Parasites</u> benefit at expense of their hosts
Singing ecolo-gy colo-gy cology

P. 35

1 - T
2 - F
3 - T
4 - T
5 - "Prey" is a noun and "pray" is a verb, so this sentence doesn't make sense. (But if the authors were being chased as prey, they would certainly pray!)

6 - E	11 - symbiosis	16 - C
7 - C	12 - environment	17 - A
8 - A	13 - biotic, abiotic	18 - B
9 - D	14 - interdependent	
10 - B	15 - number	

19 - An animal is an organism but may be a host to many different kinds of other organisms, such as parasites. To these parasites, the host is a habitat. Example: dog and fleas.

20 - A pond is a habitat for many organisms. All the organisms in the pond make up the pond community. The organisms, together with the non-living factors combine to make the ecosystem of the pond.

DIGGING DEEPER

1 - parasitic—the lice benefit and the humans are greatly irritated.

2 - mutual—both the fungus and moss benefit

3 - commensal—humans benefit but chickens don't

4 - mutual—humans get milk, dairy cattle are fed and cared for.

P. 36 ECOLOGY PART 2 - Lyrics
Plants make the food and they are producers
Animals that eat them are consumers
Eaters of dead things are scavengers
Bacteria and fungi are decomposers

Chorus:
Ecologic'ly the energy flows
Round and again the cycles goes
From the sun to autotrophs
To interdependent heterotrophs

The plant-eaters are the herbivores
The meat-eaters are the carnivores
If they eat both then they're omnivores
And that is what you and I are, of course
Chorus

Falling water is precipitation
Liquid to gas is evaporation
Which from a plant leaf is transpiration
And turning back to clouds is condensation
Chorus

There's cycles involving nitrogen
Carbon dioxide and oxygen
Loose in the atmosphere and then
In soil, plants, animals and back again
Chorus

P. 37	7 - C	13 - Plants	18 - D
1 - F	8 - D	14 - nitrogen	19 - H
2 - T	9 - A	15 - denitrifying	20 - A
3 - T	10 - B	16 - dew	21 - G
4 - T	11 - F	17 - Oxygen	22 - B
5 - T	12 - E		23 - E
6 - F			24 - C
			25 - F

DIGGING DEEPER

1 - A food chain shows how one organism becomes food for another, such as a plant for a rodent, and a rodent for a coyote A food web is more complex, showing how one organism becomes food for several others such as a plant becoming food for a rodent, or a caterpillar, or a rabbit. A rodent and or a rabbit may be eaten by a coyote, but the caterpillar would more likely be eaten by a bird.

2 - The amount of pesticide chemical consumed by an animal remains in that animal. A predator eats many insects, rodents, or other animals that have the pesticieds in them and the chemical accumulate, or become more concentratd in the body of the predator.

. P. 38 BIOMES - Lyrics
Deserts are dry but the temperature varies
Tundras are dry, but all year it may freeze
Grasslands get more rain and may be called prairies
Savannas are grasslands that also have trees

Chorus:
Oh the biomes are regions with similar climate
   (precipitation and temperatures)
The climate determines soil and vegetation
Which then determines the kinds of creatures

In coniferous forests there are conifer trees
Needleleaf evergreens like pine and fir
Deciduous forests have trees that drop broad leaves
Rainforests are wet and warm most of the year
Chorus

The freshwater biome includes streams and rivers
Lakes, ponds, swamps, marshes, and lands that are wet
The saltwater biome, the seas and the oceans
Called the marine it's too large to forget
Chorus

P. 39	6 - G	14 - Climate	22 - D
1 - T	7 - B	15 - natural	23 - E
2 - T	8 - E	16 - crops	24 - A
3 - F	9 - A	17 - annuals	25 - C
4 - F	10 - H	18 - perennials	26 - B
5 - T	11 - C	19 - savannas	27 - G
	12 - F	20 - lianas	28 - F
	13 - D	21 - prairies, steppes	

29 - tropical rainforest, also called equatorial rainforest

30 - monsoon rainforest, also called tropical deciduous forest, or tropical moist forest

DIGGING DEEPER

   The climate affects the kinds of clothing and shelter people need. The climate and soil affects the kinds of plants that grow, which determines the kinds of food people produce, and what foods they will need to import or export.

   Some of the ways humans have been able to live in different biomes include: the use of air conditioning, heating and irrigation, the ability to transport goods, and the ability to communicate quickly and easily.

Lyrical Learning